RADICALLY RESTORE MARRIAGES
IN YOUR CHURCH

THE
MARRIAGETEAM
SOLUTION

Al and Autumn Ray

ISBN: 0578192632
ISBN-13: 978-0-578-19263-5

MARRIAGETEAM
PO Box 873086
Vancouver, WA 98687-3086
(866) 831-4201
www.MarriageTeam.org

DEDICATION

This book is dedicated to the visionary pastors who have adopted the MarriageTeam coaching program as an effective approach to strengthen and save marriages. They partner with MarriageTeam to equip lay couples with marriage coaching skills and refer couples in need to MarriageTeam with amazing results. Countless changed lives and intact families are evidence of how the Lord works when pastors and lay couples serve together in His name.

PREFACE

. . . in my 37 years pastoring I got a bit jaded and cynical about para-church organizations. I avoided their pitches like the plague. It seemed to me that they always wanted my church to add something that we weren't planning on doing and frankly it seemed like they wanted to fish in my pond for financial support and my precious volunteers.

But I have found MarriageTeam to be different. I honestly believe this ministry would be a valuable asset for all churches. ~ Steve Fish, Retired Pastor

Having a great marriage may be as simple as recognizing that husbands and wives begin marriage with different playbooks. We each come from a different team called our family of origin. From our families and life experiences, we create an individual playbook for life that includes our expectations, how to communicate, handle anger, respond to conflict, solve problems and other interpersonal skills. When we marry, we create a new team; however, we bring our individual playbooks with us. Any team will have problems if it does not operate from a common playbook, and marriage teams are no exception. With a little coaching, couples can create a common playbook for a winning marriage.

The purpose of this book is to address a pressing need in the church to strengthen and save marriages. When marriages fail, families are divided. This creates emotional, economic, and social havoc as each partner, their extended families and the church all try to cope with the death of the marriage. Pastors are placed in the extremely difficult position of trying to restore the marriage and save the family, often with limited time and resources.

During a pastors' forum about marriage ministry, one pastor described marriage counseling as a black hole sucking his time and energy away from other members of the church and other duties. Another lamented that by the time a couple sought help, the relationship was broken beyond repair.[1] Other concerns around marriage counseling included:[2]

- Feeling he should take on the counseling because the couple came to him.
- A couple feeling "brushed off" if referred to a counselor.
- Reluctance to make referrals because of poor results.
- Counseling was a least favorite duty for many.

Dr. Steve Stephens, Christian psychologist, counselor, and author of more than 28 books on marriage and family, concurs with these concerns. He has identified several additional issues associated with pastoral counseling.[3]

- It creates a dual relationship as the pastor also takes on the role of counselor. Couples may be embarrassed and after counseling leave the church.
- Counseling can consume a lot of the pastor's time in an already overloaded schedule.
- The pastor can be seen as taking sides, and if there is a divorce or separation, it can create divisions in the church.
- Counseling is not a passion or strength for some pastors.
- Counseling can be overwhelming and exhausting.
- Counseling can open the door to issues that the pastor is not trained to deal with. These issues can include abuse in all its forms, addictions, mental health, legal, and medical to name a few.
- Some seminaries do not provide adequate course work for pastors to be effective marriage counselors.

Dr. Stephens goes on to say that while pastors have the best intentions, counseling, especially long term counseling, may have detrimental effects that outweigh the benefits. To protect the congregation and pastor, while ensuring couples get the best resources for their situation, he suggests an alternative approach. In this approach, pastors use their counseling time for triage and assessment and then refer couples to appropriate resources. This enables the pastor to manage the situation while mitigating the issues.

Amazingly, more than 85% of the couples who have contemplated divorce decide not to divorce after MarriageTeam coaching. <u>Its success is based on teaching effective relationship skills and facilitating the application of those skills.</u> This process creates empathetic understanding and mutual agreements on how to work together in marriage. Lasting life change is the result of couples meeting over a period of time with well-trained coaches in a compassionate, supportive environment while learning and practicing effective relationship skills. MarriageTeam coaching not only provides the pastor with effective options but also reduces the counseling workload for the pastoral staff.

CONTENTS

1

THE PASTORS' DILEMMA

If you are a pastor, I know that you feel the pain when you see couples in your congregation divorce, and all of us have experienced that [4] ~ Dr. Gary Chapman, author of *The Five Love Languages*

If you are reading this, it is likely you are a pastor or involved in marriage ministry at your church. I suspect you can easily relate to Dr. Gary Chapman's pain of seeing couples divorce.

As a pastor/ministry leader, you are God's designated representative in your church and that carries a heavy burden of responsibility for the spiritual welfare of the people in your care. You prepare couples as best you can for marriage and officiate at the wedding knowing there will be difficulties that can cause many marriages to fail. Personality differences, hurtful words and actions compounded by poor communication grow from frustration into bitterness. As an observer, you likely see this bitterness and frustration between couples in your congregation every week. Before long, their dream of "living happily ever after" has turned into a nightmare as they grow distant from each other and from the Lord. The stress and strain of career demands, unmet expectations, children, financial or health issues, in-laws and personal differences become overwhelming and they reach a point where they decide it is too difficult to stay together. Eventually they come to you with all their issues expecting you to give them the "magic pill" that will heal their relationship.

Of course there is no magic pill, and you know if they aren't able to forgive and reconcile, they will probably divorce and one or both will leave the church. Their children will be devastated and the odds are significantly increased that they will act out their loss. Statistics show that children of divorce and non-marriage are:

- Thirty-two times more likely to run away [5]
- Twenty times more likely to be incarcerated [5]
- Fourteen times more likely to commit rape [5]
- Ten times more likely to abuse drugs and alcohol [5]
- Nine times more likely to drop out of school [5]
- Six times more likely to commit suicide [6]
- Five times more apt to live in poverty [6]
- Three times more likely to be expelled from school [6]
- Three times more likely to have a child as a teenager [6]
- More likely after divorce to experience early sexual activity, hostile behavior and depression. [7]

According to an eight decade study that began in 1921 by Dr. Lewis Terman, children of divorced parents are 44% more apt to die early. In fact, parental divorce during childhood was the single strongest social predictor of early death, many years into the future. [6]

The breakdown of the family with all of the consequences is an overwhelming burden to carry. You may wonder, "What can I do to help these couples achieve a rewarding marriage that is glorifying to God and witnesses to the church and community that God brings dead marriages to life?"

You have an entire congregation to lead and limited time and staff to deal with marital issues. You desperately want to help, but know from experience that long term healing is unlikely to come from a few counseling sessions. You have probably made referrals to marriage counselors with varying degrees of success. You may even have asked another couple to meet with the troubled couple and "walk with them" through this difficult period. For some couples, this may be enough to get them back on track, but for many it only delays the inevitable separation and ultimate divorce.

Thus, you have this dilemma. You desperately want to help but you do not have the time, or perhaps the training, to spend hours in counseling sessions and still meet the other needs of your congregation.

2

WHAT IF

Through this process, we grew closer to God and each other. The tools were useful, however the relationship we built with our coaches really helped tie things together. Before coaching, our conflict was very heated and there were a lot of hurtful lies, mistrust and lack of communication. We are now praying more together and reading the Bible more often. ~ Karen

What if there was a way to help couples work together to resolve their differences and really understand each other's wants and needs?

What if there was a way to help 85% of those couples who are seriously moving toward divorce to reverse course and create a rewarding marriage?

What if all this could be accomplished taking virtually none of your time or your staff's time?

You may be thinking, "What's the catch?" Let's take a look at how all this *can* be accomplished.

3

THE PLAN

We are so excited about the results our coaches are having; we are planning to train more couples this fall. I am excited to finally have a coaching system that allows lay people the opportunity to rescue hurting marriages and to have coaching couples who I can, with confidence, hand off hurting marriages to—knowing that this process gives this couple the best chance for marriage success that I am aware of. ~ Ed Wilgus, Pastor, Sutherlin Family Church

The plan is a lot simpler than you might think. The beauty of the plan is that it also addresses one of your other major responsibilities as a pastor—to equip His people for works of service so the body of Christ may be built up (Eph 4:12), *and* it takes virtually *none* of your time! How can it get any better than that?

The plan will:
- Provide high quality, MarriageTeam coach training for selected lay couples in your congregation.
- Provide an effective referral resource for you and your staff.
- Prepare engaged couples for marriage by developing improved relationship skills.
- Strengthen, save, and restore struggling marriages.
- Yield the benefits of strong, healthy marriages and families in your church and community.

You may be thinking, "This sounds like a lot of time and effort."

Let's address this common concern before going any further. MarriageTeam is a highly recommended ministry that:

- Has proven results in its testimonials [Appendix C].
- Specializes in providing high quality training for Christian couples to become effective marriage coaches.
- Interviews couples you refer to ensure that coaching is an effective method of assistance for them.
- Provides referrals to other resources if coaching is not recommended.
- Administers the PREPARE/ENRICH inventory for all couples. [8]
- Matches your couple with competent coaches.
- Provides coaching support and ongoing training for your coaches.
- Communicates with you about the status of your couples in coaching.
- Tracks results and continuously improves services.

Consequently, it takes virtually none of your time or your staff's time to take advantage of the MarriageTeam program. The ministry is designed to support you as the pastor and leader of your church by equipping your people to serve your people. It is like having an "in-house" resource with none of the associated costs of management time and stress. Your congregation members provide the ministry and receive the blessing of seeing lives changed; your church reaps the rewards of a reputation where marriages are saved, lives are transformed and God gets the glory. This is how it works.

Phase One

The first phase is to provide high quality coach training for couples in your congregation. You can either sponsor a coach training event with other churches in your area or send couples to training in Vancouver, Washington. The 24 hours of training is normally completed during two consecutive weekends (Appendix A: Typical Training Schedule). MarriageTeam training includes a manual and workbook to facilitate learning:

- Ten relationship skills (active listening, speaking effectively, making agreements, managing anger, forgiving, resolving conflict, solving problems, appreciating differences, cultivating intimacy, achieving goals).
- Six coaching skills.
- A proven coaching process.
- How to interpret and facilitate discussion of the PREPARE/ENRICH relationship inventory.
- How to facilitate coaching sessions for premarital and married couples.

Training also includes five coaching sessions to practice newly learned skills with another couple.

Training could also be accomplished in a three and a half day retreat format. More than 500 couples have been trained with overwhelming, enthusiastic recommendations. Participants' comments include *"training was the best two weekends of our 40 year marriage"* and *"I learned more about my husband than I had in 32 years of marriage"* (Appendix B: Additional Coaches' Reviews).

Chad Hall, a Master Certified Coach and Director of the Western Seminary Coaching Certification Program explains that coaching is about asking questions, really listening, and helping the other person(s) process their situation so they can come to new awareness and resolve their own situations. The MarriageTeam training and materials are all designed to facilitate coaching as Chad explains it. Marriage coaches help couples come to new awareness and provide the relationship skills they need to resolve their own situations.

Perhaps one of the most interesting insights and testimonials about MarriageTeam training comes from Steve Fish, a long time pastor who admits to his skepticism. He shared the following thoughts with fellow pastors:

One thing I've experienced since retiring is that I can get pretty nostalgic looking back at all the years of pastoring, remembering all the incredible things God let me be part of, especially in the lives of others.

But then there's all the heartache – some of the greatest being the marriages that broke up and resulted in divorce. Like you, we tried everything to save them and build strong marriages and families. We did marriage classes, marriage weekends, sent people to seminars and retreats. I did some pastoral marriage counseling but that was mostly triage until I could pass them to someone more qualified than myself – to professional counselors and therapists. But frankly, that counseling seemed like a mixed bag and was mostly unsuccessful at salvaging troubled marriages.

This year my wife got a job with a non-profit ministry. She had been unemployed for a bit so we were quite happy. But then I learned in order for her to learn what the ministry does, she would have to go through their coach training, and I would have to go through it as well, since coaching is done as a couple.

Based on the training, I honestly believe that this ministry would be a valuable asset for all of your churches. Here's why:

- The training in Vancouver, WA does not cost anything. It is offered two times a year and is free to the participants with a free will offering at the end. [There are costs for training at other locations].
- It fits our model of ministry well: "Everyone gets to play." Coach couples are trained and deployed to make a huge difference in the lives of others. There are extensive training materials, workbooks and the program is laid out for them, as well as ongoing support from the ministry office.
- It takes the burden off you and your staff. It is a very successful program.
- It is biblically sound. You don't have to worry about the "therapist's theology" or the counselor advising the couple to do something you would not

approve of. Coaches help couples solve their own issues based on sound biblical principles. It's not therapy and doesn't focus on past hurts that are better left for counselors and therapists. It is future focused and very pragmatic. Couples learn to diffuse unhealthy emotions and arrive at healthy solutions going forward.

- I wish I had these tools years ago.

Needless to say, I was very impressed. The ministry trains lay couples to act as coaches for troubled marriages. These coaches are not counselors – as a matter of fact, they are trained not to give advice. They simply coach couples in the coaches' own home to communicate effectively and give them the tools to resolve conflicts and arrive at mutually agreed upon solutions.

Phase Two

The second phase is to refer couples for placement with your trained coaches using your new referral resource (MarriageTeam). In some circumstances, you may want to ask for coaches who are *not* in your congregation. The MarriageTeam staff interviews each couple to ensure coaching is the right approach. You are notified if coaching is not the best approach and referrals are made to the appropriate resources. Situations that are not appropriate for coaching include abuse, untreated addictions, ongoing adultery and untreated mental health issues including depression. Nevertheless, coaching is appropriate for most couples. Dr. Steve Stephens, a licensed Christian counselor, has said *"60 to 70% of the couples who see me could benefit from marriage coaching and do not need to see me."* [9]

MarriageTeam provides ongoing support for its coaches and continuing education to improve coaching skills and effectiveness. Your coach couples are actually volunteers for MarriageTeam which provides added protection for you against some of the risks identified in the preface.

Bonnie Sloat, a MarriageTeam coach and a Nationally Certified Counselor with a Master of Science in Counseling Psychology and a former Instructor of Christian Marriage at Taylor University shares some of the factors that contribute to MarriageTeam's effectiveness.

- Coaching is not done individually. Couples are matched with coach couples, which helps both husband and wife feel "represented."
- The couple invests some time with a small amount of homework and money in the coaching process.
- The couple signs a commitment with the ministry and their coaches to attend sessions, do their homework and meet regularly.
- There is implied accountability to their coaches as well as accountability to each other that is created by the coaches.
- Coaching occurs in a home setting vs. a clinical setting therefore it is less threatening and more relaxed.
- Coaches are free to spend more time with the couple in each session (typically 2 to 3 hours vs. a 50-minute counseling session).

After completing MarriageTeam coach training, Pastor Don Hallworth at Journey Church (Bend, OR) wrote this for other pastors:

This ministry is the best tool I've seen to release couples in our churches to be trained to help facilitate stronger marriages. Through significant training, ongoing support mechanisms and well written communication tools, you can have great confidence that hurting marriages in your church will receive Biblically rooted help. I have never experienced such a practical resource to strengthen marriages as the program that this ministry offers.

Bob Carlson, Senior Pastor of Brush Prairie Baptist Church (Vancouver, WA) shares about his experience with MarriageTeam.

We recently had three couples complete coach training. Almost immediately MarriageTeam was able to facilitate good matches with couples seeking help so that the coaches have had a very positive coaching experience. MarriageTeam has helped us as a church to better serve our community with a very genuine marriage outreach. Their marriage coaching model also helps us link older and younger couples together so that we can open up opportunities for intergenerational connection and blessing within our church family. I heartily recommend coach training and this ministry model to other pastors and churches. The effectiveness of MarriageTeam has opened up new ministry opportunities to members of our church and freed our pastors to devote more of our time to other ministry needs.

Phase Three

The third phase is to experience God's miraculous work as He uses your coach couples to restore broken marriages and prepare couples for marriage. You will experience the results of lives changed forever.

Amy from Portland, Oregon shares her story about her parent's divorce and ultimate restoration.

Growing up, I didn't understand everything that went on in my parent's marriage, but I was aware of tension at times, especially as I grew older. I remember as a teenager trying to keep the peace between them - always coaching my dad on what not to say, so he wouldn't upset my mom. Sometimes they would go for days without talking. The thought of them divorcing crossed my mind at times, but I always figured they would work it out.

I remember the week of Valentine's Day, 2009. My dad came to stay with me in Tulsa, Oklahoma during my last year of college. We were sitting on the couch in my living room when he told me the divorce was finalized. I was crushed, and all we could do was cry together. I knew it was coming, but reality finally set in and my heart ached for them both. I constantly worried about them. I wondered if they were lonely. Were they really happy? Eventually I was able to accept things as they were and my depression faded. One day five years later my dad and I were having a conversation when he told me that mom asked him if they could meet for breakfast and talk. He was so excited and I was so nervous. I remember telling him not to get his hopes up. At the same time I was praying that his heart wouldn't be broken when mom tells him she just wants a friendship.

I was at work the morning they met for breakfast. Mom called me afterwards and said, "How would you feel about your dad and me getting remarried?" I was in shock and asked if she was serious. She said they had a long talk and agreed to let the past be the past. They were going to do things right this time. They were going to attend marriage coaching which came highly recommended by our church. The thought of sitting down to discuss their relationship with strangers made them both a little uneasy. However, after their first meeting they told me they were paired with the perfect couple! They felt so comfortable and were looking forward to their next session. Their coaches were nonjudgmental and provided an atmosphere where my parents could be completely open. They didn't spend time talking about past issues but worked on moving forward to build a positive relationship for the future.

On June 13, 2014 my parents remarried. Never had I imagined them remarrying or even dating again. It was so far from my mind. I didn't want to get my hopes up, but my heart was filled with so much joy. Although I was a little nervous for them, I felt at peace because they had both grown so much in their personal relationship with God. I knew this was Him giving them a second chance. Now, I see them use the marriage coaching tools and their communication is so different! The blaming is gone. They do not brush things under the rug or go for days without talking. Their relationship is not perfect, but they are able to have an actual conversation, be respectful, not dwell on things, but move forward.

I never expected to be telling anyone this kind of story. I didn't want to be like my parents. I was afraid of a relationship—not to mention marriage—but it did give me hope to see how God was working in their lives and how marriage coaching was changing them.

Six months later, I met the man I was to marry. Naturally, my parents recommended premarital coaching and my wonderful fiancée agreed. We liked the idea of working with a Christian couple instead of a counselor. Our coaches helped us learn skills while keeping God at the center. This was especially important to my fiancée and me because we wanted to be obedient to God and confirm that our marriage was in God's will—not just ours.

Through marriage coaching, we discovered we needed to learn and to use good relationship skills to have the foundation for the kind of marriage we both wanted.

We are so grateful that God provided this ministry. It has truly changed our family.

Other shorter testimonials are captured in Appendix C.

4

HOW DO I GET STARTED?

*This training went beyond my expectations. . . . we got a
very organized, step-by-step, repeatable program (that
relies on the Holy Spirit) with great support and a
curriculum that works.* ~ MarriageTeam coach

The easiest part of implementing this plan is to get started. You
can refer couples for coaching even before you have any trained
coaches. In most states, MarriageTeam offers long distance, video
coaching, which is as effective as coaching in person. To request
coaches, couples contact MarriageTeam directly via an online form
found on the website (www.marriageteam.org), calling (866) 831-
4201, or emailing info@marriageteam.org.

To learn more about the training program and how to equip
couples in your church and community for effective marriage
ministry, contact MarriageTeam.

In closing, Dr. Gary Chapman has the following insight to share:
A few years ago, I met the founders of a ministry called
MarriageTeam that trains lay couples to be marriage
coaches. MarriageTeam will take couples in your church,
and every church has at least one couple who has a passion
for marriage, and it will train them so that they come back
and you have someone that you can refer couples to who
are struggling. I want to challenge you to check it out. I
think you will find this to be a great partner for you and
your ministry.[4]

ENDNOTES

1. Pastors' Round Table Discussion, Royal Oaks Country Club, Vancouver, WA, February 3, 2011.

2. Pastors' Forum, US Digital Outreach Center, Vancouver, WA, August 19, 2014

3. Dr. Steve Stephens, telephone interview, March 5, 2017.

4. Dr. Gary Chapman Video, recorded at Calvary Baptist Church, Winston-Salem, NC, May 5, 2014.

5. According to the Census Bureau, the Centers for Disease Control and Prevention and the U.S. Department of Justice as reported by https://thefatherlessgeneration.wordpress.com/statistics

6. McManus, Mike, *Ethics & Religion*, Children Are Hurt by Marriage Failure, Column #1,824, August 10, 2016.

7. *Choosing Wisely Before You Divorce*, Church Initiative, PO Box 1739, Wake Forest, NCF 27588-1739, 800 489-7778

8. PREPARE/ENRICH is an online assessment for married and unmarried couples who want to understand and improve their relationship. Over three million couples have used the assessment to help them clarify their challenges and make specific positive changes. A great deal of research has helped make the assessment extremely effective.

9. Radio Show, Portland, OR, KPAM 860, Interview with Dr. Steve Stephens, May 22, 2011.

ABOUT THE AUTHORS

Al and Autumn Ray were married in 1970 and are the founding directors of MarriageTeam, a non-profit that trains Christian couples as marriage coaches and provides marriage coaching services. Together they authored Rick and Jane Learn to Listen and Talk describing the marriage coaching process. Al retired from the Air Force with his last assignment as the Professor of Aerospace Studies at the University of Portland. He has a Master of Science in Counseling and Human Development and Autumn has a Bachelor of Science in Social Work. Autumn retired from Multnomah County Department of Community Justice where she was the Volunteer Manager. They both completed the Western Seminary Transformational Coaching program, are a certified Marriage Enrichment leader couple, Seminar Directors for PREPARE/ENRICH and skilled trainers. They have two children and two grandchildren.

APPENDIX A

TYPICAL TRAINING SCHEDULE

Day	Start	Finish
Friday	7:00 pm	9:45 pm
Saturday	8:30 am	4:00 pm
Sunday	1:00 pm	5:45 pm
Saturday	8:30 am	4:00 pm
Sunday	1:00 pm	5:45 pm

ALTERNATIVE TRAINING SCHEDULE

Day	Start	Finish
Day 1	8:00 am	5:00 pm
Day 2	8:00 am	5:00 pm
Day 3	8:00 am	5:00 pm
Day 4	8:00 am	noon

AL and AUTUMN RAY

APPENDIX B - COACH TRAINING REVIEWS

I would like to extend a very heartfelt thank you. We love each other very much but that wasn't enough. I would like you to know that we actively practice and use the tools and methods we learned in the training. Rarely does a day go by that we don't put them into active practice. Even when the principles aren't communicated verbally, they are on our minds and in our hearts. We came into the training not intending to become coaches but have since realized what a wonderful thing coaching is. Our marriage has benefitted greatly because of your ministry and we are happy and moving forward. Husband

What I loved about the training is that the coaching process starts working immediately in the first session. I love that the process allows for clear and safe communication with the focus on listening and understanding my teammate. The program doesn't allow couples to dwell on problems but leads them to explore new options of interacting, which guides them to resolutions, improving the relationship immediately. Wife

I am armed with tools and I learned that I don't need to have the answers. What a relief! I can use coaching tools to help the distressed couple find their own answers. Husband

I could feel the presence of the Holy Spirit working. I appreciated the openness and the ease of presenters. The Coaching Manual was well done. I liked that we were not rushing to get through the material. Wife

This training went beyond my expectations. As we started, I anticipated just getting some tools to use if we found someone who needed coaching. What we got was a very organized, step-by-step, repeatable program (that relies on the Holy Spirit) with great support and a curriculum that works. Husband

I liked that even though we are talking about very serious subjects there was levity with the training. The training creates a safe environment which allows you to share openly for maximum benefit. Wife

I am leaving this training with a sense of "I can DO THIS! I can help to coach other couples!" The material makes sense to me. It has a logical and practical system and flow that builds positive communication and personal growth. Husband

The process equips non-professionals to make a difference for families through the help of the Holy Spirit; that is POWERFUL! Wife

I came hoping to improve my marriage and learn to help others; Mission Accomplished! The materials and concepts presented were outstanding. The coaching experience was very beneficial. I really appreciate the "heart for ministry" the trainers have. Thank you for answering God's call. Husband

This training exceeded my expectations. It's so effective and easy to implement and has a straight forward structure. I loved that we were given lots of practice! I gained skills and insight that I can take away today and use with my family, friends and co-workers. I was able to tell everyone about the process with ease because it clearly works and could help everyone! Wife

I enjoyed the practice coaching sessions to sharpen our skills. The ability to process with different couples really reinforced learning the skills and program for me. Being coached by other couples, enabled me to experience the process of being coached, which allowed me to appreciate how effective coaching can be immediately in changing the dynamics and set patterns in a marriage to produce constructive outcomes. Husband

The manual is written so well. It is very easy to understand the step-by-step lesson plans. Husband

What an absolute privilege and joy to be a part of the recent Marriage Coaching Training. As ones who have had training in counselling before and are actively helping marriages from many different sides, the training couldn't have come at a better time. It challenged us to think in some new ways with others and also gave us some great time to look at our own marriage and go forward in some needed changes. The training has already been very beneficial as we've talked with others! Dan and Laura, Poland

We are super excited to think about all the marriages in Slovakia that, the Lord willing, will be impacted as a result of the marriage coach training we received. Our own marriage of 28 years was greatly affected and revitalized in just 3 1/2 days of the training. Thank you for generously investing in our lives and in the many couples we hope to begin coaching soon. Mark and Amy, Slovakia
c
We had no idea what to expect when we came into the marriage coach training, and we honestly wondered whether we are at all qualified to do this. But the training far exceeded what we could anticipate. Not only did we have to wrestle with hard spots in our marriage, but we learned how to coach other couples to go deeper in their marriages too - without having to give them the answers. Instead, we learned how to get couples to talk to each other and listen actively. It was encouraging, empowering, and inspiring. We are ready to start immediately with coaching couples in the Czech Republic. Brian and Aleisha, Czech Republic

Marriage coach training was very significant for us as a couple as well as the leaders of the Slovak team. Training helped us to dig out the issues we needed to address many years ago. It helped us to move on in the area of trust, communication and our different personalities. What a joy to be closer to each other as well as to have a great tool to help the other couples. Peter and Eva, Slovakia

APPENDIX C – COACHING REVIEWS

Our coaches really worked hard on making us use good "I" statements. They went back to these often with us so that we would apply this good skill. Before coaching, we did not communicate, and if we did, it did not go well and did not resolve or accomplish anything but more strife and tension. Since coaching, we have returned to date nights. We have realized how far off our relationship of oneness had strayed from what God intended. I try to work on being more loving towards my spouse. Bridget, Mobile, AL

I appreciated that our coaches helped us get to root causes that caused so much hurt, pain and frustration with each other. They were amazing facilitators with the process. Before coaching, I was researching divorce, there was high tension between us and I was completely done with the marriage. I was only in it for the kids. Now I understand much better my husband's needs and motivations. I see how my words and actions (positive and negative) affect my husband's spirit. Joan, Salem, OR

The coaching was excellent and helped my wife and me work through our difficulties with new communication skills. My wife had moved out more than a year and half before coaching and if she did not agree to coaching, I was going to proceed with a divorce. We had a great lack of communication and could go a month or more without speaking. She was living 45 miles away. Both of us were very hurt. Our relationship is like we are starting over or new. Because we have changed the way we communicate and view each other, it's like we are getting to know each other for the first time. However, this time we are much more patient and understanding with each other. I find myself not getting frustrated with my communications with my wife now. It's not perfect but, we are learning how to work through situations that used to be very stressful that are now typified with patience. Dale, Seattle, WA

Having been through counseling before and previous divorces, we both had some curiosity about what coaching would entail. My husband was resistant because he didn't want it to be a one sided "pick on the husband" session. Coaching was extremely helpful! This gave us tools that will help us for the rest of our lives. We now have a much stronger foundation and a better way to approach communication on a long term basis, with goals and plans for the future together. Alyssa, Eugene, OR

When they were arguing and fighting, I would wish that it would stop soon, because I didn't like hearing it. I would sit in my room and read to get my mind off the fighting. I was afraid they were going to separate. One morning they came in and woke me up and said they were going to MarriageTeam today. So they started going every week and I started noticing the change. They don't fight like they used to. It makes me feel relieved, so I think that it is a really good thing and that married couples that are having problems should try this because it makes a really big difference. It helps the kids too. Maddie, teenager, Vancouver, WA

For us the coaching experience was incredibly helpful and helped us to diagnose and fix issues that we had struggled with for a very long time and didn't know how to approach. Coaching has provided better tools for communication between me and my spouse and we are able to speak more effectively to each other. The coaching process led us to self-discovery and thru that process it will stay with us much longer and produced a lot more fruit. Also on deeper levels there was soul care which really touched us deeply. They helped us see problems that were not just skill related. It was a very comprehensive experience with our coaches. Daniel and Iwona, Poland

Our coaches provided us with an excellent professional service with a personal touch. We appreciated they had a strong Christian background. We found the sessions to be non-biased but very pointed as to identifying the problems. The process required both of us be willing to take responsibility for each of our contributions to conflicts. Our relationship was very tense before coaching. There were a lot of hurt feelings because we each had our own way of trying to communicate and get our desired outcome. The biggest change that we've experienced since coaching was a fundamental shift in our approach to solving problems and communicating. After coaching both of us realized neither of our strategies were helpful in finding a solution that we both felt good about. We are continuing to work on improving communication and intimacy, but we feel like we now have the tools to attempt such behaviors in a more effective manner. Jane, Dallas, TX

My experience in coaching was awesome. Never would I have guessed that I would have enjoyed it so much. I would do it all over again. Our relationship before coaching was rocky. We were letting our pride get in the way. We are now much better at working out arguments. To improve your program, you should advertise more. People need to know how great it is. Todd, Springfield, OR

I never thought this method would work but after the first session, I was committed. Before coaching, we were caught in a vicious cycle of arguing and blaming each other. Now, we hardly argue and if we have a disagreement, we use our tools to work it out. Even our three girls have noticed we hardly argue at all. Steve, Ridgefield, WA

Coaching helped us discuss issues in our marriage where we felt tension but were not able to discuss them and come to some solutions on our own. We are very thankful that with coaching help we were able to discuss these issues and resolve things that we weren't able to do on our own. Drahoslav and Zuzana, Slovakia

Our relationship before coaching was awful. We were in the first months post my husband's affair. Coaching was great! Not easy at times, but very valuable and worth the time and effort. We were considering divorce before coaching, but have decided not to divorce as a result of coaching. Jane, Vancouver, WA

We realized some issues we needed to work on, but we didn't know how to work on them. Our coaches have helped us to meet God in the process and to realize this is a huge benefit for us. Coaching created the breakthrough of our married lives. Gelu and Lydia, Romania

For 14 years I spent all my time trying to change my husband into who I thought he should be instead of letting God work on me and learning how to let go and let God. Before coaching, I felt hurt, resentment, anger, bitterness and hatred toward my husband. I did not feel love and I did not show love. As a result of coaching, I have learned how to communicate with my husband, listen to my husband, value his feelings, understand him and most importantly how to show him I love him through my actions. Misty, Mobile, AL

Our coaches were supportive, entertaining and knew what to say, or not say at just the right time. It was a very positive experience and really was the turning point in our marriage. Before coaching, we were at a breaking point, unhappy and didn't know where to turn. Now we have less anger and we are communicating in a positive way. Eileen. Vancouver, WA

I was a little skeptical about working with a couple. The material and concepts were much better than anything I have been through before. Before coaching, we were struggling to communicate and understand each other. It was causing a lot of negative interaction between us. Our communication has greatly improved. We feel much closer than before and have been able to tear down walls. Eric, Camas, WA

Coaching was great and exactly what we needed. We had been to counseling but knew we needed ongoing help. The tools really work and our coaches were amazing at pinpointing where we needed extra work. Before coaching, we were struggling with very little trust and a lot of pain. Now, trust is being rebuilt as we see each other trying. Jes, Portland, OR

Coaching really helped us learn new skills. It was great and we really enjoyed it. Before coaching, our relationship was not good. My wife was always attacking me verbally. I didn't want to go home. We are now working toward a good marriage. Shane, Mobile, AL

Our experience was successful and enjoyable. I loved being able to bond closer to my husband by using the steps we learned. Our relationship before coaching was disappointing, unfulfilling and very empty. We now have better communication, more respect and forgiveness. Lauren, Eugene, OR

Prior to coaching, divorce came up as a frequent topic. We've learned real applicable tools to help with daily life as well as working through conflict. We have decided not to divorce as a result of coaching! Heather, Portland, OR

I learned what emotional intimacy is and how to practice it with my wife. It is her biggest need and I was completely missing it. Before coaching, we were on the verge of collapse. We were angry and frustrated. Now we enjoy spending time together and anger has substantially diminished. Steve, Vancouver, WA

The MarriageTeam material covered every single topic that I wanted my marriage to grow in. We have fewer fights. Most of our fights are ending before they start, because we communicate in a way where we understand the other person and are able to diffuse a situation before emotions escalate. I also feel more loved, and my husband does not shut down anymore. My husband also has gained a lot of confidence and is much more open. Jane, Vancouver, WA

The coaching process was hard but good. It was hard to dig deep for the answers, but incredibly healthy and beneficial. Jordan, Vancouver, WA

Our coaching experience has helped so much. Before coaching we were very disconnected and didn't know how to talk to one another. We would bottle up our feelings and leave each other guessing about how one another felt. We really learned a lot about each other and how to communicate much more effectively. Nicole, Portland, OR

The coaching sessions were super insightful for me and super beneficial. I realized some really key things that I was absolutely stuck in. The coaching sessions really helped me get unstuck and understand why we couldn't communicate well because of previous issues. Dusan and Dana, Czech Republic

Our coaches created a safe environment for us. I could find easy solutions that were not so easy when just me and my wife were talking about these things because we always have some baggage with us. Mart and Greta, Estonia

My husband would not have been open to counseling. This was a much better format. Before coaching, I was very angry with him because of unresolved problems. I would yell at him out of frustration. I'm yelling less now as we are trying to use what we learned to communicate more constructively. Susan, Corbett, OR

The observations of our behavior and manners were usually spot on – and we were given insight into why we may be feeling that way. Our coaching experience was very good. They were very accommodating of our schedule. Our relationship before coaching was tense. I am now becoming more comfortable expressing my feelings and "volunteering" information I would usually keep silent with. I have already recommended this program to others. David, Vancouver, WA

I thought that coaching would simply be advice and tips, but was wrong. By being able to work through issues directly with the coaches and practice the skills in front of them, we were able to achieve immediate changes. The coaches were extremely knowledgeable and helpful. I really enjoyed and benefitted from it. Before coaching, we didn't talk about most of our problems. We were unable to share feelings in a positive manner. I didn't want to spend time with my wife. Now, I genuinely want to spend time with her and time working on our relationship. We are both able to communicate and listen more effectively. Husband, Hillsboro, OR